$f\mathbf{P}$

AND ONE MORE THING BEFORE YOU GO...

Maria Shriver

Free Press

NEW YORK LONDON TORONTO SYDNEY

f**P**

FREE PRESS
A Division of Simon & Schuster, Inc.
1230 Avenue of the Americas
New York, NY 10020

Copyright © 2005 by MOS Enterprises, Inc.
All rights reserved,
including the right of reproduction
in whole or in part in any form.

FREE PRESS and colophon are trademarks
of Simon & Schuster, Inc.

For information regarding special discounts for bulk purchases,
please contact Simon & Schuster Special Sales at 1-800-456-6798
or business@simonandschuster.com

Designed by C. Linda Dingler

Manufactured in the United States of America

10   9   8   7   6   5   4   3   2   1

Library of Congress Cataloging-in-Publication Data is available.

ISBN: 0-7432-8101-2

Dedication

───── ❧ ─────

To my mother, Eunice Kennedy Shriver. You have always been my greatest champion. Thank you for your love, your wisdom, and your example. I love you, and I admire you. To my amazing children, Katherine, Christina, Patrick, and Christopher, and my remarkable husband, Arnold. I love and adore each of you with all of my being. XOXO.

Oh . . . and one more thing . . . I also want to dedicate this book to all of the extraordinary mothers that are serving on the front lines of humanity! You have my deepest respect and admiration.

Contents

Contents

Acknowledgments

———— ❦ ————

This little book wouldn't be a little book if it weren't for my friend and mentor, Roberta Hollander. Everything my mother didn't teach me, Roberta did, and then some. She pushed me to do this speech and to turn it into a book. Then she kept at me when I kept saying, "I don't think it is good, I don't think it is long enough, I don't like it, no one else will like it, I don't have time to do it." She has held my hand through all of my struggles and she holds it still. I love her, and I thank her for sharing her life lessons with me.

To my colleagues, Teri Hess and Sandra Wareing. I couldn't write anything if you didn't work with me, support me, and encourage me in everything I do. Thank you from the bottom of my heart for putting up with me. To Jan Miller and Shannon Miser-Marven, my adored agent and wonderful friend. This is our fifth book together. I value you and admire you both. To Camille McDuffie. I wouldn't know how to do a book without you. To Martha Levin and Dominick Anfuso. I don't know if you know it, but you took a risk hooking up with me. I hope it pays off for you. And finally, to all my remarkable, loyal, funny, wise, and loving girlfriends. You sustain me in such a deep and profound way. I love you all, and thank you for all the lessons you have taught me.

Introduction

---✿---

You know what used to drive me nuts when I was a teenager? Just when I was dressed and had one foot out the door, my mother would inevitably say, "And one more thing before you go . . ."

Needless to say, it was never just one more thing. It was more like five or ten. "Don't drink. And don't get in the car with anyone who has had a drink. And Maria, one more thing. Did you tell me where you're going? Why are you going there? Oh, and one more thing. Be home by your curfew. You do know when your curfew is, right?"

Even today when my mother calls me, we talk

and talk, then say good-bye, and two minutes later she calls back to say—you got it—"One more thing, Maria . . ."

That's a mother for you. So of course, now that I have four kids, *I'm* the one who says, "And one more thing before you go." *I'm* the one with daughters rolling their eyes and plugging their ears.

Which brings me to this little book. It grew out of a speech I gave at a sweet mother-daughter luncheon for high school seniors and their moms. My good friend Ally, a graduating senior, invited me to speak. I also wanted to support her mother, Wanda, one of my best friends, who was a wreck, because Ally's going off to college three thousand miles away from home. (Her brother had already committed the same crime.)

At the luncheon, there were a couple of hundred girls with their mothers, all of them at an emotional crossroads—which of course is what high school graduation is.

What I hoped to do for the mothers that day was articulate many of the things they wanted to tell their daughters—and probably what I want my own daughters to know as well, even though they're each a few years away from The Big Day. (I've already wept quietly at their elementary and middle school graduations.)

Afterwards, many of the moms urged me to package the speech into a little book.

So voilà! Here's a little gift to all my comrades in motherhood—and to their daughters, who will, to their horror, grow up to be just like us. Ha! Gotcha! (Only kidding.)

This is pretty much what I said that day—adding a little here and there, because after all, you've paid for it. And at the end, I've added some words of wisdom a few high school senior daughters I know want to pass along to us moms.

So . . . off we go!

I've thought a lot about what I could say to you.

You're not children anymore, so I can't read you one of my children's books (although they are worth reading!).

I don't want to talk to you about broadcast journalism, because I'm not doing that for the time being. (Don't get me started on that one.)

I'm sure you all could give your own speeches about what's going on in college nowadays—and all the cool technological gizmos that connect you and your laptop to the university and the rest of the planet. So you won't be hearing that stuff from me.

I considered telling you what you need to know before you enter the cold, cruel world out there. But I already wrote that in my book, *Ten Things I Wish I'd Known Before I Went Out into the Real World.*

Besides, college *isn't* really the real world. But neither is high school. So that's my topic today:

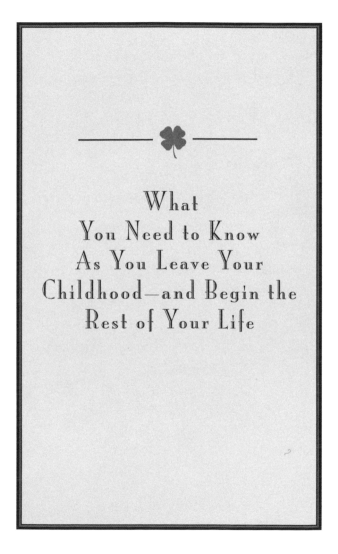

What
You Need to Know
As You Leave Your
Childhood—and Begin the
Rest of Your Life

1

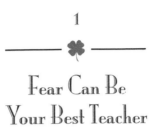

Fear Can Be
Your Best Teacher

I know a lot of you sitting there are plenty fearful of what's coming next—college, the big wide world, the unknown.

Well, trust me on this: it's okay to be scared. And not only is fear okay, it's a *good* thing. Our fear gives us wisdom. It lets us know we're confronting something new.

Fear lets us know what we don't know. It tells us

we may need help. We may have to keep our eyes open. We may have to learn the ropes. We may have to stay awake and aware.

So just because you feel afraid, doesn't mean there's something wrong with you. It's okay to be nervous about the big leap you're about to make— away from your cocoon of familiarity in high school and at home.

Someone once told me not to be afraid of being afraid, because, she said, "Anxiety is a glimpse of your own daring." Isn't that great? It means part of your agitation is just excitement about what you're getting ready to accomplish.

And whatever you're afraid of—that's the very thing you should try to do. I always tell my kids, if you're afraid to jump into the twelve-foot water, you'd better jump right in. Or as Eleanor Roosevelt said, "Do one thing every day that scares you."

And don't think you're weird because you're scared. If it makes you feel any better, I was scared when I graduated from high school. I was afraid when I graduated from college. I was a wreck when I went to work at my first TV station. I was terrified when I anchored the national news the first time. (In fact, I ran to the bathroom and threw up.) My legs shook when I walked down the aisle to get married. My voice cracked when I said my vows. When I gave birth for the first time, well, there isn't even a word in the dictionary describing that kind of fear. Even in my forties, I get scared. I get anxiety before every book of mine is published. And when my husband was elected governor of California and I became first lady, I experienced rolling waves of panic.

But the bottom line is this: I made it through all these things. You jump in, you do it, and you come out the other side. In fact, I believe the fear of the unknown helped me, because fear is a great motivator. It makes us work harder than we imagined we could. It makes us think outside the box— which is the only way you can do anything original and exciting in life.

Here's one of my other favorite quotes, and this one I have on a T-shirt: "Well-behaved women rarely make history." Well, guess what? Neither do women who are ruled by fear and play things safe.

So even if you don't plan on making history, remember: Fear is normal. Fear is common. And it keeps coming back.

BOTTOM LINE

As you dive into your own future, remember this: If you feel afraid, it means you're alive. That's good. Now use it.

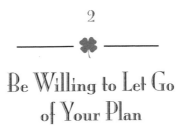

2

Be Willing to Let Go of Your Plan

Now, to manage or even eliminate your fear of the unknown, you may think you've got everything all figured out. You're going to this college, and this is going to be your major, and you're going to get that job, and then X years later, you're going to get married to Y kind of guy—and on and on. It's your Master Plan.

Girls, I thought I was the *master* of the Master Plan.

When I was your age, I just knew I wanted to make a name for myself outside the family business, which was Democratic Party politics. Politics? Forget that! My passion was broadcast journalism, and my goal was to be a network news anchor.

I started at the bottom and worked and sweated and sweated and worked—and I can't emphasize this enough—worked my butt off to get to my goal. And I got there. Check one off on the Master Plan.

My plan also included picking a husband waaaay outside my family's expectations for me. *They* wanted Washington, politician, Democrat. I picked Austrian, bodybuilder, Republican. Bye-bye, Nation's Capital. Hollywood, here I come! Check another one off on the Master Plan.

Oh, yeah? Well, look what happened to me! It turned out the Austrian Republican decided he wanted to go into politics—and on his first try, he became governor of California. Talk about whiplash. My head did a 360 on my shoulders.

And what did *his* job change mean for *me*? Everything. It meant an end to my job as a broadcast journalist, because people were worried about a conflict of interest between the issues the governor deals with and the stories I would do. Believe me, quitting my twenty-seven-year career in television was *not* on my radar. But you will experience in life that sometimes *your* plan isn't everyone's plan. Guaranteed, your life will get derailed at some point, like mine did.

And *then* what? Was my world over? Well, frankly, it did feel that way for a couple weeks. But I didn't want to live with that feeling—resentful and so rigid that I couldn't handle change.

So what did I do? Well, I had to be flexible. I had to be willing to stop whining about and move in a new direction. As they used to say in the sixties, I had to go with the flow.

I told myself it only *felt* like the end of the world, because I had laid out my world in a very, very specific way. But it *wasn't* the end. It was just the beginning of the next phase. My very best friends assured me, "Your life isn't over. It's just altered." Remember that phrase: *just altered*. It'll come in handy in your life.

So here's the lesson for you, too: Be willing to make changes. For instance, right now you may be quite thrilled with the college you're going to. Well, surprise: you may not love it there. You may want to transfer. I did that.

And right now you may be excited beyond words to be leaving home and striking out on your own. Well, maybe next spring you'll decide you'd really be happier closer to home. Did that, too.

Maybe you've known since you were ten that you wanted to be a doctor. Well, what if you fall in love with writing and want to be a novelist? I didn't do that one. I just knew I didn't want to be a nun.

BOTTOM LINE

Don't lock yourself up and throw away the key. Don't be so rigid that you can't change your plans. Be willing to change, to adapt. Be willing to switch direction and strike out on a new path if you want to. Or if, like me, you have to.

3

Learn from Your Mistakes

Now, not being afraid of fear—and being flexible and willing to deviate from your Master Plan—means that you might make some mistakes. Great! If you don't know that it's okay to make mistakes, let me teach you that lesson right now.

Who's not going to make any mistakes? Only the person who doesn't try anything she doesn't already know. Come again? I said, if you want to avoid making any mistakes whatsoever, then you can't ever try anything new. Is that who you want to be? So small-minded, so stale, so narrow in your focus, so scared to look bad?

Let me tell you something. In my life I've had to be willing to fail, willing to look like a fool—in other words, willing to learn. If you don't know how to do something, you have to learn it. And learning usually includes making mistakes.

I've made a lot of mistakes along the way. In fact, in my new job as first lady of California, I just made a doozie. A biggie. And it came back and bopped me on the head. Let me explain.

To make a long, boring story sort of short, I started helping a small, failing museum in Sacramento, California's capital. It's a private museum in a public building, and it was running out of money. I was asked to help.

I launched a wonderful multimedia exhibit called "California's Remarkable Women," honoring everyone from the earliest settlers of California to aviator Amelia Earhart, from Jane Stanford to Dianne Feinstein, from farmworker organizer Dolores Huerta to Venus and Serena Williams, from Elizabeth Taylor to the creator of the Barbie doll.

The exhibit was a great success, everyone came, and it got a lot of press. There were streams of new visitors to the museum for the first time in a long time. Everyone was happy. So far, so good.

Then the board said, "Since our museum is going bankrupt, come up with another idea, or we'll have to close our doors."

I said, "Let's just turn the whole place into a permanent California Women's Museum. There's nothing like that in the whole state. We'll be able to do something that isn't being done: tell the story of California through the eyes of its women. Great idea?" The museum board apparently thought so and voted overwhelmingly for it.

And here comes my doozie. Because I was so impatient, because I didn't do my homework, I forged ahead.

I come from journalism, where you run with a hot idea before somebody else can beat you to it. Now I was in a new job with new rules, but I didn't know what they were—and I didn't know I didn't know. Which is no excuse, because I didn't consult anyone either.

So before I had the time to pat myself on the back, *whammo!* It hit the fan. Instead of taking bows, I started taking heat. Headlines in the papers went something like this: "First Lady Exercising Muscle." "Shriver Taking Over Museum." "Three Museum Board Members Resign."

All of a sudden I was Cruella de Vil. Certain state legislators wanted to know who the heck I thought I was. Letters to the editor firmly reminded me that it was my husband who was elected, not me. I was accused of railroading the board and hijacking the museum.

Oh, man. I was in a foxhole—and when you're in a foxhole, you're in it alone. All of a sudden I seemed to have offended everybody, no matter how good the idea was.

You see, there's a proper way to do these things, and I hadn't bothered to find out what it was. I was in a new job, with a new cast of characters, new rules, new sensitivities. If I'd have done my homework, I'd have learned that it wasn't enough that the museum board loved my idea. I should have slowed down. I should have talked to people in the legislature. I should have gotten other opinions and suggestions and built a consensus.

Luckily, I've made plenty of mistakes in my life, so I didn't panic. I just started digging myself out of the hole. I wrote op-ed pieces in the newspaper to explain what I'd been trying to do. I put my ego aside and started talking to people I should have talked to before, looking for common ground.

After a few months of going back and forth, we came up with a new idea that worked for everyone: turning the failing museum into the California Museum for History, Women, and the Arts—which will finally tell the story and history of California women. We were able to move forward because I communicated, I listened, and I ALTERED—there's that word again!- -my vision. In other words, I got because I gave.

So just because you make a mistake, don't think you're finished. Don't panic. Do admit it. It's not the end of the world and not even the end of your life. Even when you become successful in your life, every time you go into a new area, you'll discover there are new rules. Lesson learned.

The sad truth is, girls and women often think they're not allowed to screw up. They think they have to be perfect. Let me tell you another thing: Perfectionism doesn't make you perfect. It only makes you feel bad about yourself, because no one can *ever* be perfect, including you.

BOTTOM LINE

Don't sell yourself short by being so afraid of failure you don't dare to make any mistakes. Make your mistakes and learn from them. And remember—no matter how many mistakes you make, your mother always loves you!

4

You'll Need a Lot of Courage

As you step out into the next phase of your life, you're going to need COURAGE. More than the No-Doz, more than the tutor and the computer—believe it or not, even more than the boyfriend!—you'll need Courage with a capital C.

That's how you're going to face your fears, be willing to change, try new things, and handle the lumps and bumps that life puts in your path.

I wrote in my first book, "Courage isn't the *ab-*

sence of fear. It's walking *through* your fear with faith." It's having the faith that you're going to be okay, even though for the moment you're scared. It's being able to plow ahead. Courage is the quality that enables you to do that.

Just look at you today. It's already taken a great deal of courage to navigate high school successfully and get to this point. Now it's taking more courage to leave home and strike out on your own. Many of you are making some big, life-changing moves. You're taking out student loans. You're taking on a new job—or even two. Some of you are the first in your families to go to college, which can be an awesome responsibility. I applaud each and every one of you for what you've done already and what you're about to do.

To continue down the path you're paving for yourself, you'll need different kinds of courage. Moral courage, financial courage, spiritual courage, even physical courage—all of these will help you meet and match every challenge you face in any area of your life.

And let's get real here. You *will* be challenged, and that's a good thing. That's how you get courage in the first place—by facing up to trouble, trials, and tough times. Right when you're struggling is *exactly* when you learn you have an abundance of courage and all the strength you need to do what you have to do to make it through.

You know, we make a great mistake thinking we're supposed to be happy all the time, that a good life is an *easy* life. Many people whose lives are easy also feel empty. If everything comes to them with no effort or struggle on their part, they're never tested. They never get to learn what they're made of.

One of the great life lessons you're about to learn, if you haven't already, is that the things you'll value most in your life are the things you have to fight for and work for and struggle for. And if you think about it, most of the *people* you admire—people you know, people you've studied, those who've changed the world—have also suffered and struggled and fought with great courage to overcome obstacles.

It's not shameful to struggle. It's not wimpy or weak. It's an important, inevitable, and integral part of life, not to be avoided. In fact, what's wimpy is avoiding the struggle in the first place.

For instance, as you move through your life,

you'll have to make plenty of choices that test your ethics and morals. There may be pressures to use illegal drugs, to cheat in school or work, to isolate or gang up on someone who's different from your group.

Struggling with these pressures will force you to make some big decisions on your own. You'll have to ask yourself questions. "What kind of ethics and morals do I have? What kind of human being do I want to be?"

If you decide to be strong and resist caving in to those pressures—in other words, to resist taking the weak and wimpy way—then you'll find you have all the moral courage you need to stand up and be the person you want to be. You'll have the strength to do what's right for you, even if it means being embarrassed in the short term. The courage to say NO will be yours.

And when you come out on the other side? You'll have struggled and won, you'll have grown, and you'll feel really great about yourself. You'll know you're a courageous soul. You're strong and true to yourself down to the core. That's *real* happiness, and no one can take it away from you.

So don't be so self-centered that you expect

everything to come to you, quick and easy on a silver platter. If that's the way you think, the first time life throws you a curveball—and it will—you'll be whining, "Hey! That's not fair!"

Believe me, it's fair. It's not only fair, it's the way life is. First you're happy, and then you go through a time of struggle. And then there's smooth sailing, and then the rough ride begins again. Over and over again. That's the way a good life is meant to be.

I know sometimes you look at certain people and think, Boy, I'm jealous! S*he's* had an easy ride! I know many people have thought that about me, because I come from a prominent family, and my husband turned out to be a big movie star. Well, folks, like everyone, I've had my share of struggle. I've been to too many funerals, dealt with so many medical emergencies, worried myself sick over parenting issues. Now I'm working with my family to support my father's battle with Alzheimer's disease—talk about struggle.

Make no mistake, I'm not whining, because this is life. My struggles and the courage I've gained through them have made me the woman I am today. I'm hoping they're the reason you think enough of me to read this book.

BOTTOM LINE

Along with love, courage is what you need more than anything in this life. In tough times it tells you, "I can go through this!" Even when it feels like you can't.

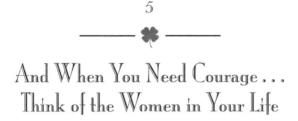

5

And When You Need Courage . . . Think of the Women in Your Life

That's right. Your mother! Or your grandmother, your aunt, your big sister—any woman who's made *your* life *her* business.

Whenever I'm in a jam, whenever I need some hope, I look to my own mother. She's my inspiration. She's my example of courage—of how to handle crisis, how to navigate life's lumps and bumps with my head held high. How to survive, endure, and triumph.

Trust me: There isn't any other job on the face of the earth that requires more courage than being a mother.

It takes great courage, first of all, just to give birth. Then it takes a big heart filled with courage to do the work required to raise children: to teach them; to give them time, attention, and direction; to help mold them into good human beings with good values.

It takes even more courage to accept who your children actually are, accommodate yourself to that reality, and help them grow into the adults they're supposed to become.

And when the time comes, it takes more courage then you can wrap your brains around to let your children go. When I left college, I made a series of really self-centered decisions to move from my parents' home in Washington first to Philadelphia, then to Baltimore, then to Los Angeles. Now I still live three thousand miles away from my parents. Never once in my wanderings did my mother ever say, "What about me? Don't go!" When I look at it now, if *my* daughter told me she was moving across the country, I'd pull my hair out. So I understand it took incredible courage for my mother not to say anything. Even today, my mother's strength and courage in every area of her life blows me away.

BOTTOM LINE

When you feel down, when you're having tough times, when you think you simply don't have the strength and courage to go through something or just to press on—think about your mother or any Important Woman in your life. Think of her strength and her courage and what she's had to go through in her life.

And it wouldn't hurt you to pick up the phone and give her a call!

6

— ❧ —

It's a Balancing Act

Have balance in your life. You may actually be the first generation to have a shot at it.

The generations of women before mine had a tough choice. It seemed to them that they had to choose between family and career. They had to pick one brass ring or the other.

If they went for the career track, they had to focus so hard on getting ahead that family was considered a distraction. If they went for the mommy track, well, that meant they couldn't possibly betray the family and do anything outside the home.

Then came my generation. And geniuses that we were, we thought we were superwomen and could have both brass rings at once. We worked full-time and had families full-time, at the same time. And we paid a huge price.

When we were spending time with our families, we felt guilty for not going to work. When we got all caught up in our work, we felt guilty about our kids. We found out Superwoman had no peace of mind whatsoever.

Well, I think young women today are savvier than we ever were. They recognize that the brass ring is *balance.* Balance means weighing and measuring your priorities to put together a life that fulfills you on your own terms, not society's expectations of you, one way or the other. And balance also means recalibrating your priorities when you need and want to. I think that's great.

So maybe you don't have to rush out and be the first woman on the moon, the first woman CEO of a Detroit automaker, or the first person who implants a computer chip into a bumblebee's brain.

Maybe you also don't have to rush out and meet

that Special Guy right away. Maybe you can take your time and balance *all* the parts of your life so that you can *have* a life.

BOTTOM LINE

Weigh out your competing priorities and see how you can fulfill them over time, without making yourself insane with guilt. If you achieve that balance, that'll make all of us older women envious of you—and proud.

7

Have a Little Gratitude

I've been reading articles about how terrible it is that many high schools these days put so much pressure on students to excel and compete and accomplish, that you kids have too much stress in your young lives. As if it's a burden to have gotten an education.

Puh-LEEZE! A little GRATITUDE!

You're so lucky. You just got the great education this country has to offer. I do congratulate you for making it through, because I know how hard it was. But you have to be grateful—to the teachers who taught you and trained you so well; to your parents, who helped give you the opportunity to have this invaluable head start in life; to your friends who've helped smooth the path for you with love and laughter.

Gratitude is a great place to be. Any time you're in a funk—or feel like you messed up and are a loser—or that good ol' standby "NOBODY LOVES ME!"—any time you feel icky like that, just make a gratitude list for yourself.

A list like this:

"I'm grateful for parents who've given me every benefit they could."

"I'm grateful for my friends, who don't think I'm a dork."

"I'm grateful to be going to such a great college."

"I'm grateful to get such a great job."

"I'm grateful for my little sisters and brothers, because they're so darn cute and some people don't have any."

"I'm grateful for my dog, who loves me no matter what."

"I'm grateful to be alive and healthy."

This list could go on and on.

Gratitude lifts your spirit. It takes you right out of yourself and onto a different plane.

BOTTOM LINE

When you're stuck in self-pity or envy or worry, try getting grateful for something in your life. It's good for the soul.

8

Keep a Childlike Quality

By that I mean stay *curious.* For instance, maybe there were subjects in high school you didn't like but had to take. (For me, the monster was math.) Well, in college very often you can slide over those nasty ones and find the areas you're curious about, dig in, and get a taste.

I've always been incredibly curious, and I found a profession that rewards it. Journalism is all about asking questions and getting answers. But you don't have to be a professional journalist to want to know more than you already do.

Bring curiosity into your life. Be curious about the people around you. My dad taught me not to project preconceptions or assumptions onto the people I met. He told me they had a lot to teach me—about where they're from, what they think, what their lives have been like. He always asked questions of people. He was always curious—and that in turn made people view *him* as gracious and charming.

If you ask a lot of questions, you'll get lots of answers. That's information—and wisdom. You won't just assume you know a person from the labels it's so easy to pin on them. If a girl is pretty, it doesn't mean she's dim-witted. Ask questions. Find out. If a guy's a bodybuilder, it doesn't mean he's dumb. Ask questions. Find out. *I* did, and now I'm the first lady of California. (Just kidding.)

This is a great gift you can give yourself as you go off to college or into the work world. Don't make yourself ignorant by resorting to quick judgments based on labels: "This kid's from the Midwest. He can't possibly be cool." Or "I never met anyone from that religion. It's weird. Better stay away."

Like a child, stay curious, stay open-minded.

That's how you'll get street smarts—the stuff they can never teach you in books.

And also like a child, stay teachable—which means knowing you have plenty to learn.

If you're going to do well in college and beyond, you need mentors. These are the guides who already know what you want to know and already know how to do what you want to learn how to do.

Mentors are generous with their time and wisdom because they see in you something of themselves, and they want to help it flower.

When you identify a subject or an area you're passionate about, often it's because you've seen that passion in somebody else, and you want a piece of it, too.

I would be nowhere in my life if I didn't have mentors and guides who walked my various paths before me. Some of them were college professors. Some were priests. Some were coworkers. These are people who wanted to help me succeed.

In a way, your parents are like mentors, because they still have a lot of information to teach you about negotiating your way through school, work, and relationships—and they *really* want you to succeed.

BOTTOM LINE

Keep part of your childhood alive in you—the part that is curious, asks questions, and is willing to find and cultivate relationships with the people who can answer them.

9

Forget Your Mirrors

Now what on earth could I mean by that? Well, I know you're all headed out to college to begin fulfilling your dreams—and God knows, I'm all for that. But let me make a recommendation. It's based on both my experience and my observation of people who love their lives.

I'll quote my father here, a speech he gave at Yale University several years ago.

He said, "I have one word of advice: Break your mirrors! Yes, indeed—shatter the glass!"

Now, don't think I'm nuts telling this to teenage girls. Listen to what he said:

"In our society that's so self-absorbed, begin to look less at yourself and more at each other! You'll get more satisfaction from having improved your neighborhood, your town, your state, your country, and your fellow human beings than you'll ever get from your figure, your car, your house, or your credit rating."

Ladies, that is the truth with a capital T. Being of service is a gift you can give yourselves. And I'm not just talking about selling cookies or wrapping paper for your church or school.

I'm challenging you today to not just join sororities in college, to not just spend your extra time in the Starbucks, although I love Starbucks.

How about joining a service organization that helps kids in your new community? How about putting in some time volunteering at a local environmental group—or a group like Best Buddies or Big Sisters that gives a hand to the mentally disabled or the economically disadvantaged?

In addition to lining up your own tutor for college-level chemistry and French—how about *being* a tutor at the boys and girls club near campus?

Right now, when young men and women are risking their lives overseas in the name of our country, how about asking ourselves what we can do to make life better for people here at home?

And when you're thinking about what to do after college, how about setting your sights really high and thinking about a career in public service? Or a couple of years in the Peace Corps or AmeriCorps or your state's service corps?

The message is simple: You want to *feel* good? Then *do* good. Being of service is a big spirit booster. It makes us feel part of the big picture on the planet.

BOTTOM LINE

Every one of us can make a difference. Everyone can be the difference in the lives of someone else. And when we are—trust me, it feels like a million bucks.

And finally:

10

Don't Worry About Us.
We'll Just Sit Here
in the Dark All Alone.

Now I'm speaking to you as a mother. When you go off to college, your mothers are going to go through an acute episode of empty-nest syndrome. That's a form of suffering you won't understand until you go through it yourself. Be compassionate and kind!

Because right now, in your adolescence, you may be resenting the fact that you've been at the center of your mother's life. You wonder, "Why doesn't she grow up already!"

Well, resenting your mother is genetic. It gives you girls some of the energy and motivation you need to get out of the nest *yourself.*

But, for your mother, empty-nest pain and grief is genetic, too. She took care of you, nurtured you, enjoyed you, is in awe of you—and now she's letting you go. How could she *not* have deep feelings about it?

Think of the alternative. Do you really want a mother who doesn't care that you're leaving? Come on! So allow us to grieve a bit for the loss of our little girls—even as we are so proud of the young women you've become.

And speaking for a moment to you mothers: I don't envy you at all. Believe it or not, I experienced empty-nest syndrome for the first time when my fourth child was first born!

There I was seven years ago, in my hospital bed holding my precious last baby boy—and I was already projecting he'd be gone pretty soon, too, leaving me all alone!

Well, reality is sneaking up on me now. This past Christmas, my oldest girl said, "Just think! I'll be decorating only three more Christmas trees with you—and then I'm outta here!" Ouch! She's fifteen. Later she said she was only kidding and just wanted to see my reaction, which was tears. But when I think of sitting at her and then her sister's graduation luncheon a few years from now, I want to puke.

But I won't. I'll just have to do what I'm telling you girls to do today: think of my mother, what courage she had to let all five of her children go out into the world—and then just be flexible one more time, as my life changes yet again. But I won't like it, trust me.

I'll be like all my girlfriends going through *their* daughters' last year in high school now. They're emotional wrecks, but they pull themselves back from the brink in an incredible act of courage at the very last moment—to help their kids pack. And *that's* the bottom line!

Okay. That's it for now.

Graduating seniors: As you sit here before your last high school summer, it's bittersweet, isn't it?

You're SCARED of going off, yet DYING to be

independent. You're EXCITED to make new friends, but SORRY to be leaving pals you've been with for years. You've heard that high school has prepared you so well that college will be a snap, but you really don't believe it.

Well, here's the real deal: You're not just leaving high school. You're leaving your childhood. Even now I remember what that felt like. It was a delicious sensation—fear-inducing and fabulous at the same time.

So, girls, I hope you enjoy that feeling of stepping out into your future.

And remember, be especially nice to your mother. She's stepping out into her future, too.

So, that's it. See, it didn't take so long.

Oh, and one more thing before you go: Have fun, laugh, and enjoy yourself. It'll be a blast.

Now, off you go!

Afterword

Since I gave that speech, I've watched more waves of daughters getting ready to go off, full of promise and potential.

I ask myself, what do I wish for all of you girls? They're the same things I wish for my daughters and myself.

My father always said to me, "Honey, everyone is lucky when you walk into a room." I hope each of you always feels confident walking into a room on your own. Know that you're enough, and you don't need a guy by your side to be okay or acceptable.

I hope you always remember that you're an

original. There's no one on this planet exactly like you. You can waste your time focusing so hard on your weaknesses that you devalue yourself and ignore your strengths. Don't minimize your uniqueness. Carry the awareness of it with you when you walk into a meeting, into a school, into a job. The conference, the college, the corporation—all of them are lucky to have you.

I hope you'll learn everything you need to know about your own money and finances, so you don't need a guy to make your decisions for you.

I hope you'll realize you don't need to become a Bill Gates or an Oprah. Become your own person. When you decide exactly what you want to do and then go after it—whether it's being a baker or running a day-care center or becoming a soprano—that is the fulfillment of your own dreams, a life beautifully lived.

Okay. Enough of what your mothers and *I* think. Here's what some of *you* think.

I asked a couple of girls who are high school seniors what they want their *mothers* to know. What would you tell your mother, if you could just get her to sit still and listen, without interrupting as usual?

Here's some of what they wrote:

ROSIE

1. I want you to be proud of our relationship and how much fun we have together. I cherish our time alone and want you to know that our bond is unique.

2. Please keep in mind that I am NOT an angel, but I am perfect when compared to many girls at my school.

3. I swear I'll keep reducing you to hysterics by saying I'm "escaping" to college if you even CONSIDER for one minute changing my room when I'm gone or, even worse, giving it to one of my four siblings.

4. When I do badly on a test or I'm mad about something that happens in the dorm, do NOT give me advice. Telling me to meet with the teacher or confront my friends is NOT what I want you to say. I want you to tell me it's okay, I worked hard, and it doesn't matter.

5. Never stop being yourself. Thank God you are such a phenomenal woman. I want you to remember that you are my role model for everything I want to be and do.

ALEX

1. Mom, it's very disconcerting to me that you cry as hard when I talk about going away to college as you do when you watch a holiday Budweiser commercial.

2. You're absolutely right that many of the times when you screamed at me, I wasn't listening. But the times we sat and talked like girl-friends, I cherished your words more than you'll ever know.

3. I have a secret to tell you: I still have no idea how to do laundry.

4. When I was little, I thought you were a magical fairy princess. When I hit thirteen, you became annoying and stupid. When I was six-teen, you were my worst enemy. Now at eigh-teen, I see you as a strong, courageous, and beautiful woman, but most of all as my hero.

5. Thank you for raising me to be the woman I am today—mature and humble enough to see you were right (most of the time).

And finally, this is from Ally, the girl who invited me to speak at that graduation luncheon. She's a college student now, three thousand miles away from home. What does she want her mom to know?

ALLY

1. Thank you, thank you, thank you. Thank you for the opportunity to go to college, let alone the school I wanted to go to most, all the way on the other end of the country. Trust me, I know I'm lucky.

2. I won't spend all your money. Contrary to popular belief, most kids do realize that when they spend money—whether on a taco or a pair of boots—it's not coming out of their own pockets.

3. This is a big one: If I'm crying, it doesn't mean I hate school. There's such a huge difference between hating school and adjusting to it.

4. If I can't talk with you on the phone, it doesn't mean I despise you. Not only do I not despise you, I love you!

5. Sometimes I'll act like I'm still your little girl. But then again, sometimes I'll think I know more than you. Please cut me some slack. After all, I'm still a teenager, and I can't help

it. The teenager of the species thinks she can conquer the world, but when faced with an obstacle, she still needs her mommy.

To which I say: Thank God.